overheard
at
waitrose

newly updated edition;
includes 30 recently overheard poems

quotes overheard in public
and transcribed by
nathan bragg
theresa vogrin

idiocratea ◗

Copyright © 2018 Idiocratea

Newly Updated Edition Copyright © 2020 Idiocratea

Cover Design and Art Direction by Nathan Bragg

Illustrations by Theresa Vogrin

Editing and Text Arrangement by Theresa Vogrin

All rights reserved. No part of this book may be used, performed or reproduced in any form or by any electronic or mechanical means, including photocopying and recording, or by any information storage and retrieval system, without prior written consent from the author except for brief quotations in critical articles or reviews.

Idiocratea is an imprint of Polygon Publishing LTD.

POLYGON PUBLISHING

www.polygonpublishing.com

www.idiocratea.com

ISBN-13: 978-1727130775
ISBN-10: 1727130774

This book is not authorised, endorsed by or affiliated with *Waitrose* or its subsidiaries.

this book
is for
all waitrose customers
who brighten up our days
with their heartfelt
complaints
concerns
statements.

keep calm
and
carry on
shopping.

contents

the
gossiping

smells strange in here today.
either the parmesan is not organic
or the state schools
have not gone back yet.

i just couldn't believe it.
she thought
the french riviera
was a continent.

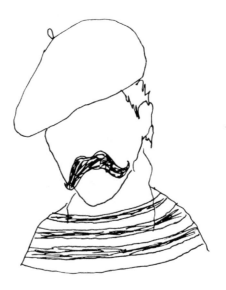

well quite frankly karen
and with respect
i could not care less
about what carol
and everybody else at church
think of my divorce.

oh i don't know
they just seem
to let any riff-raff in here nowadays.
it's starting to look
like the local tesco express.

i couldn't believe
that poor lass thought
val-d'isère
was a cocktail.

i would never accept
anything less than
an inquisitively laid egg
on my breakfast table.

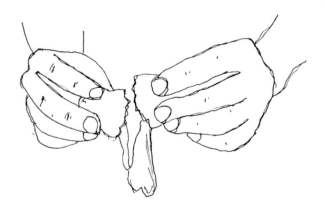

i don't know
why they have
own-brand in here.

i mean
you just wouldn't
show your face
at the till
with that butter.

i know
i just died
when they offered me
a ferrero rocher with my bellini.
rough as tits it was.

absolutely rough as tits.

it was business class
and they didn't even
have peppermint tea.

i was speechless.

i really need
to cleanse
my chakras.

are you having
your annual swinging soirée
again this year?

last year's was a hoot.

i honestly do not see
the appeal in love island.
absolutely feral behaviour.

it's like world war 3
in this godforsaken place today.
it's christmas
not the bloody apocalypse.

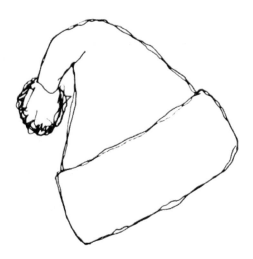

i'm going to
the bahamas next week.
trying to decide on
which cleanser to pack
is actually *really stressful*.

i would have a breakdown
but i've got a facial
booked at 2pm.

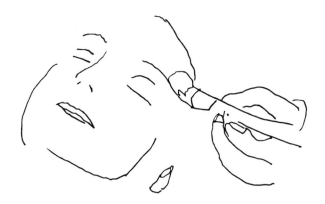

you mean to say
you eat an apple
with your bare hands?
without a knife and fork?

how liberating.

since they started
to offer free coffee
it has been
like a soup kitchen
in here.

i have
the school run
french horn practice
and a personal training session.

who could possibly work and have kids?

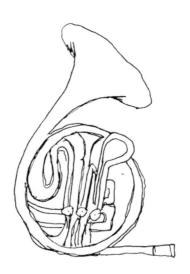

i would cook scampi for dinner
but i just don't feel
i could do it justice
after the way our butler
cooked it on holiday.

this place
is going downhill.

they don't even
have peacock food.

they don't even have
raw cacao powder.

it's like
the back streets
of russia
in here.

of course
i would buy
the smoked salmon
but it makes
the maserati
smell like a fishmonger's.

oh come on
as if you would ever
see me on the tube.

ghastly thing.

no i'm not a snob
but people who aren't rich
disgust me.

don't use
the leaf blower
when you are wearing
a scarf.

i nearly
hanged myself.

well
that's the last time
i'm doing anything
to support the working class
after this is how they have repaid us.

i'm terrible.
i came in
for rose essence
and activated charcoal
and i've left with a basket full.

i don't know
how i survived
thirty-five years
without slimline elderflower tonic.

it really is
a taste revolution.

i'm ashamed to admit the fact
that I snuck a copy of *the sun*
inside my copy of *the independent*
to read katie hopkins' column.

i'm so poor at the moment
i'm having to go on a budget.

are you going to start shopping
at tesco or asda then?

oh darling
i'm not that poor.

one doesn't have to be posh
to be privileged
darling
but it sure does help.

people knock
the european nannies
but by god are they cheap.

the paper quality
of waitrose christmas cards
doesn't seem to equal last years.

brexit must have hit hard.

no i told you
i can't drink red
as i have just had
my teeth whitened.

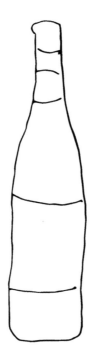

you can forget
our weekends
away to cannes
now that
the selfish working class
have voted
to leave the eu.

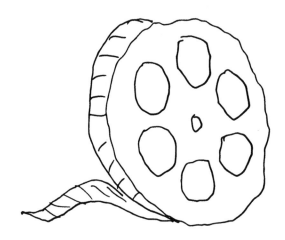

harry asked for a corsa
for his 16th birthday.
we did our research
and got him an audi instead.
just to learn in.

it looked a lot safer.

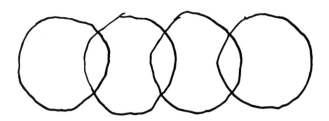

i know
she is my daughter
but her paintings are appalling.
her use of greens
is one of the few saving graces.

the
loving

mummy
what does
extra virgin oil mean?

it means that
it's the best kind of oil
darling.

am i an extra virgin son?

henry
you can't have
those kumquats.
look at the air miles
they have travelled.

this is for dad's dinner.
pay attention
you'll have to cook
for your husband
one day.

- mum to daughter

haven't we had the discussion
about shoving things
down the front of your trousers
in public?

do you want to choose
some sweets?

no daddy.
i want brie and crackers.

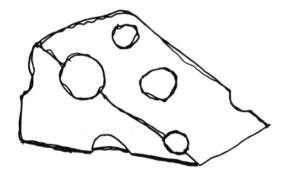

darling please
don't slouch
like an old lettuce.

stand up straight.
you have
the posture
of a gorilla.
stop making
a fool of me.

mummy
will we have to sell
some of the holiday homes
now that we have left
the eu?

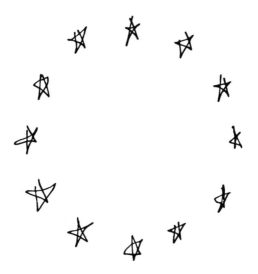

yes darlings
i know you have chicken pox
but mummy
must get bits
for the dinner party
or she'll be a laughing stock.

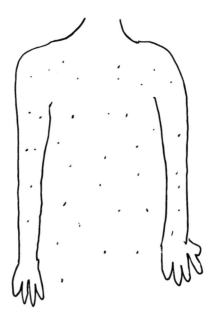

when in doubt
just choose
the most expensive one
oscar.

it has served mummy well
with daddy.

mummy
what are those things
next to the star fruit
and lychees?

they are called *apples*
darling.

anais
don't hit your brother
with the veal steaks.

can you go
and get my umbrella
out of the car
so i don't get wet?

                                        it's not that far?

i know
but this is
a cashmere cardigan.

darling
what have i told you?
it's bay-zil
not baz-il.

you're making a fool of us.

why non-organic apples
darling?

stop making a fuss.
they're for the horses.

mummy
when are we going
back to oxford?

brighton is dirty.

i told you
before we left the house
that people would stare.

- woman looking at her husband's socks and sandals

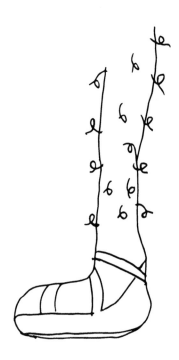

papa
does *merlot* have a silent *t*
just like *mortgage*?

poppy i don't care
what francesca's parents
bought her.

you're not having another pony.
look at poor darcy for lord's sake.

shall we buy
a tin of performative biscuits
or some biscuits
we actually want to eat?

which house
are we celebrating
christmas in this year?

elijah
put those down.

i've told you
what kind of people
eat crisps.

cashews and goat's milk
in our basket?

for the squirrels
of course.

don't forget
the cashmere enriched
toilet roll
darling.

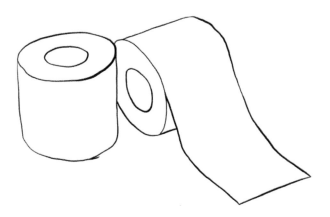

nanny
that's a brioche
not a pain au chocolate.

it's prosciutto ham and asparagus
for packed lunches this week.
did you want tarte au citron too?

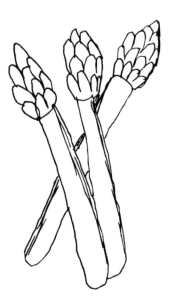

you look so obnoxious
when you do that.

please stop
it really isn't attractive.

- woman to her nail-biting husband

oh darling
throw a few of those in.

they are increased price
and will make us
look expensive
at the checkouts.

if it's not organic
i'm not eating it.

it's rather quite simple
when you think about it
mummy.

- *little girl to her mother*

papa
please can elise and i
have some violet truffles?
mummy said we could
if we were well behaved.

please
don't rummage
in the reduced bin.

darling
someone from the golf club
might see you.

what type of bread
would you like
to dip into your mussels?

- *mum to her two kids*

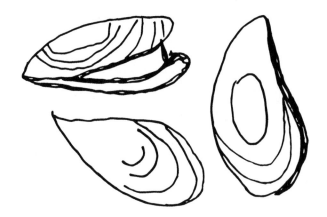

darling
they only have five varieties of brie.

i told you
we should have gone
to the oxford branch.

samantha
put that *essential* stuff down.
when i married you
we agreed not to compromise
on the quality of our balsamic vinegar.

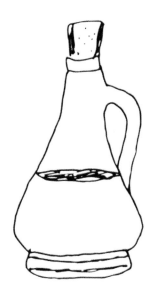

i hope nanny
doesn't get drunk at dinner
and embarrass us all again
like she did last year.

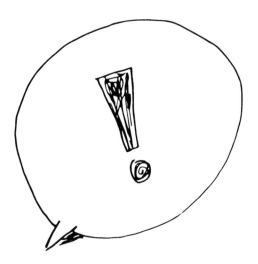

pop the charity coupon
into one of the boxes.
just nothing to do
with the homeless or gypsies.

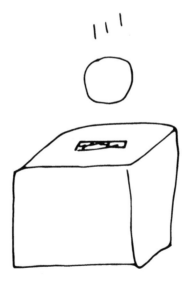

it's hardly
fortnum and mason
but since daddy
put me on a budget
i'm having to cut back.

darling
can you grab
some organic blueberries
for the gerbil?

simon
don't get the basic hummus –
you will make
a laughing stock of me.

just put two
in the basket
otherwise we will
look greedy.

yes i know
it ruins everything
but they have run out
of fresh cranberries.

no there's none
in the grocers either.

well karen
what do you want
me to do?

bloody grow them?

- man on his phone

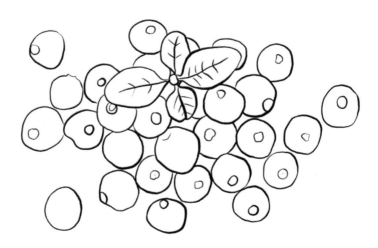

put
the daily mail
down
right this instant.

daddy said
we are not going away
until the annual family ski trip
in september.

i can't go that long
without a holiday.
it's criminal.

you will like potatoes
darling
it's what gnocchi is made of.

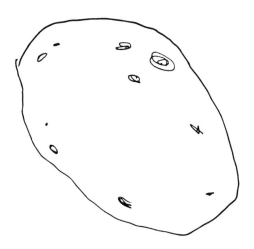

go and give the change
to the big issue seller outside please
and don't make a meal of it.

buy two.
it will make us look
more expensive
darling.

would you run back to the car
and get my fitbit?
i'm doing
a daily showdown
with catherine.

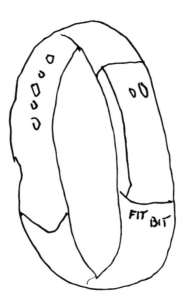

darling
give the change
to the sad lady
dressed in brown
at the entrance.

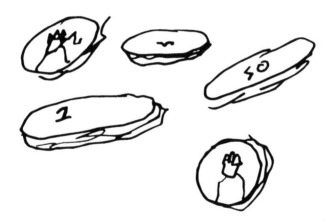

no we can't go
to marks and spencer.

our cat
will only eat
salmon from here.

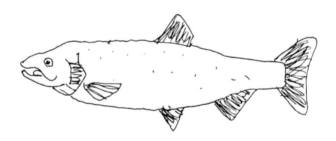

oh buggery-botch-wagons.
felicity
do mummy a favour
and grab the organic quinoa.
quickly darling
before it's our turn to be served.

the
pestering

yes madam
basil
thyme and oregano
are in aisle two.

no darling
i'm looking
for my children.

i'm not impressed
by the number of seeds
in your *easy peel* clementines.

do these rubber gloves
come in lilac?
it's such a chore
having to do the dishes
whilst our dishwasher
is on holiday.

perhaps you'd like to tell
my daughter
why her packed lunch cencioni
is without fresh pesto?

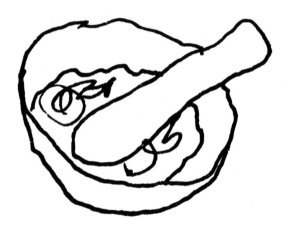

how do you expect me
to serve a soup
at my dinner party then?

there is always a soup to start.
there will be a riot.

well i don't understand
how you can't have
organic courgettes.

what is this?
east berlin?

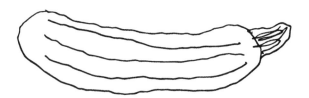

over here.
chop chop.

- man at the self-service checkout needing assistance

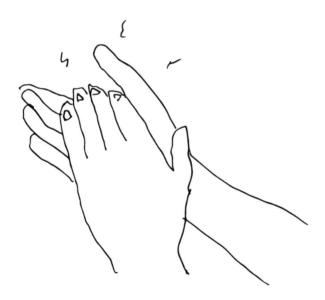

the woman's voice
on the self-scan machines
sounds so impolite.

- customer complaining to staff member

security here.
there's a customer
with a pet rabbit in a cage.
is it allowed
in the store?

i called
and your colleague
explicitly said
they were in stock.

perhaps
you would like to explain
to my daughter
why her fondue evening
is ruined?

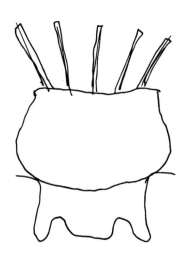

well
what do you suppose
i do with this focaccia
if there's no bloody olive oil?
hmm?

would you like
a free take-away drink?

only if it's
a gin and tonic.

i just found
a live snail
in my strawberries.

do you even wash them?

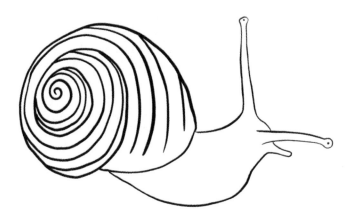

your range
of quails eggs
is fairly limited.

where is
the free range
weetabix?

excuse me
do you stock
the earl grey chocolate thins?

i either got them
from here or selfridges
and i can't remember
for the life of me.

oh actually
can i swap
that bag of organic hibiscus?

i can see a fruit fly.

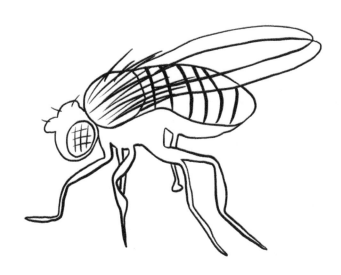

no boxes
for the champagne?

am i supposed
to levitate them
to the car?

have you got
any non-alcoholic alcohol
for non-alcoholic drinks?

do you mean alcohol?

no.

can i talk to you
about the provenance
of your sheep's yoghurt?

if you were
a discounted mop
where would you
want to be displayed?

- *a member of staff*

my daughter is on the phone.
she would like you
to explain the reason
why the fresh fruit pouches
she needs in her lunch box
aren't here.

i need to read
the numbers
on the barcode
aloud to you.

i don't want any lasers
touching my food.

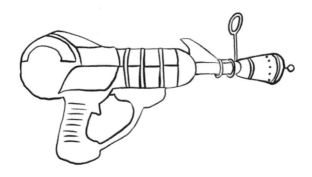

very well then.
frozen lobster
will just have to suffice.

perhaps you'd like to explain
to my guests
why waitrose
only had enough foie gras
for five people?

this is a staff announcement.
there has been a champagne spillage
in aisle four.

oh no
my mistake
everyone calm down.
it's only cava.

would you like a bag?

well what do you think?
do i look like
i need a bloody bag?

i wish to make a complaint.
waitrose is getting
too cheap.
if i wanted cheap
i would shop
in lidl.

if you enjoyed
overheard at waitrose
please consider leaving
a review on amazon.

thank you.

other books published by *idiocratea*:

overheard at waitrose II
overheard at whole foods
google search poetry
milk and brexit

about this book

overheard at waitrose is a collection of the most iconic quotes overheard in *waitrose* stores and posted across social media platforms like twitter, facebook and instagram under the meme name *overheard in waitrose*.

idiocratea does not hold the copyright to the words, only to the illustrations and the presentation of the quotes.

our only intention with this book is to make people laugh and brighten up their day.

about *idiocratea*

idiocratea is an imprint of Polygon Publishing LTD. with our constantly expanding selection of trendy mugs, meme related products, gag gifts, personalised items and our very own range of original books, we at *idiocratea* pride ourselves on selling extraordinary gifts for extraordinary people.

check us out on instagram (@idiocratea_ and @polygon.publishing) and don't forget to browse our stores at **www.idiocratea.com** and **www.polygonpublishing.com**.

about the contributors

nathan bragg

nathan bragg is a uk-based digital marketing specialist, entrepreneur and lover of memes.

theresa vogrin

theresa vogrin is an austrian writer, living in the uk. she published her debut poetry book *Bitter-Sweet* in july 2018.

check out theresa's work on instagram (@theresa_vogrin) and facebook.

Printed in Great Britain
by Amazon

15083166R00078